YOUR WORLD
AND THE BEAUTY IT BEHOLDS

YOUR WORLD
AND THE BEAUTY IT BEHOLDS

EXPLORING THE WORLD
THROUGH MOMENTS AND LANDSCAPES

ANDY PIÑEIRO ROMERO

Dedicated to all.

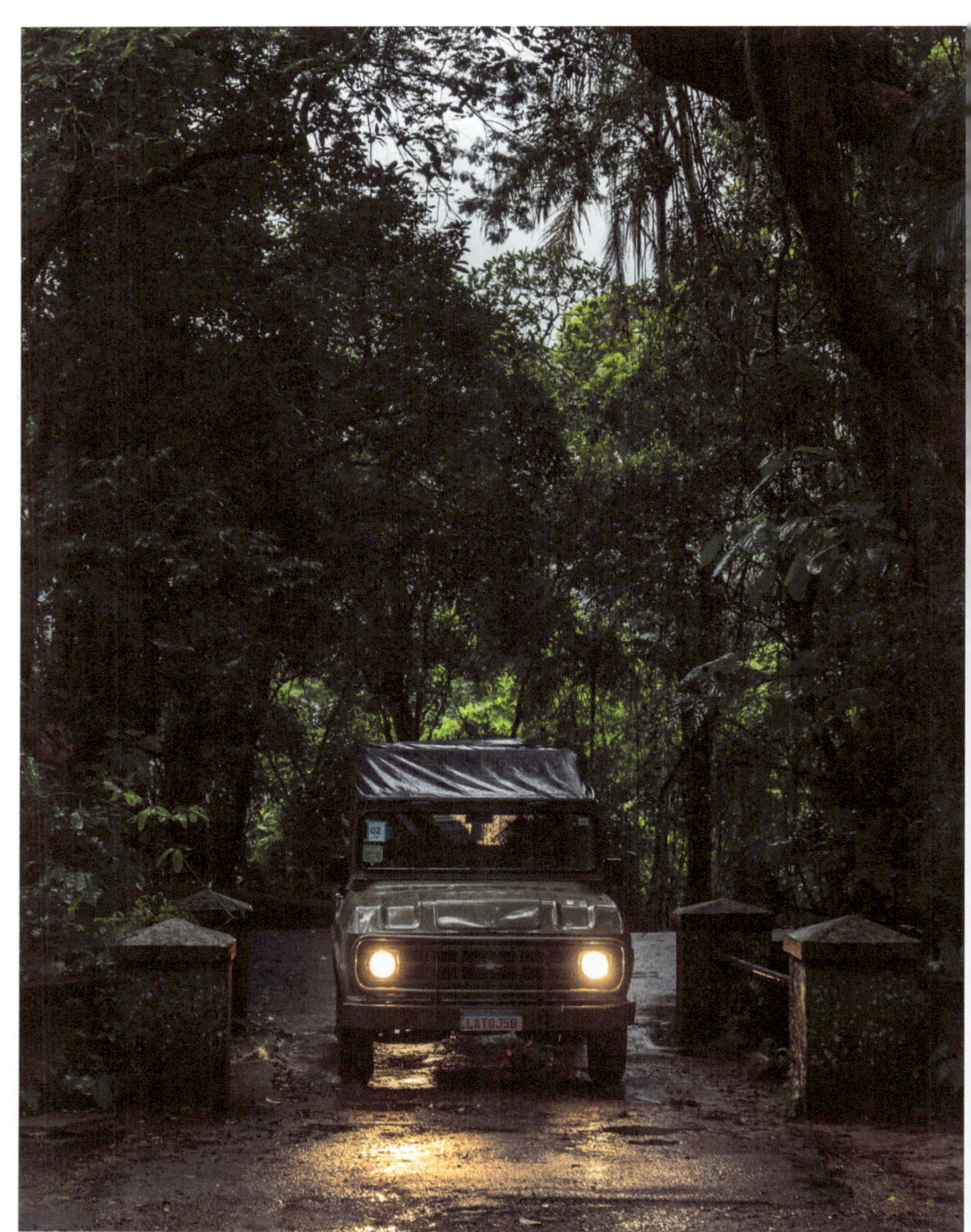

Tijuca National Park, Brasil

YOU WERE DROPPED IN A MASSIVE GLOBE.

GO EXPLORE IT

You only get one opportunity to take a good glimpse at it. To share what you see and how you feel, to get your feet dirty and see places you wouldn't imagine did exist.

BECOME A TRAVELER

In an ever-changing world, travelers bring stories and new ideas — new perspectives and ways of life. A traveler is always interesting.

MEET THE STRANGERS

They'll give you stories and lessons to remember. Introduce you to new ideas and ways of looking at the world. And leave you with unforgettable memories.

ENJOY THE JOURNEY

Savor each moment you have — watch as the wind wrestles with the leaves and the sun cuts through the trees. Listen to the songs of nature. Take a breath of fresh air and live.

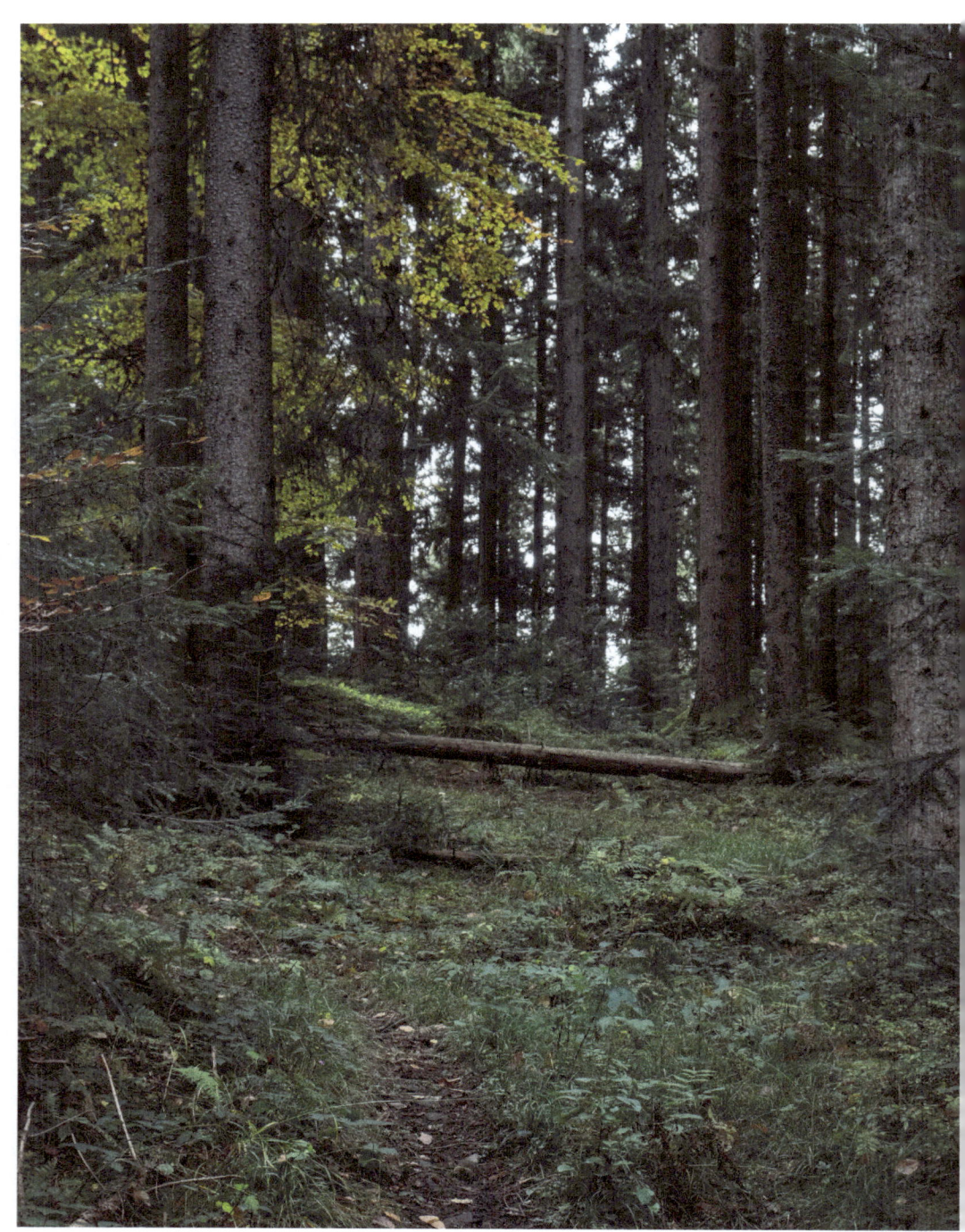

Gindelalm, Germany

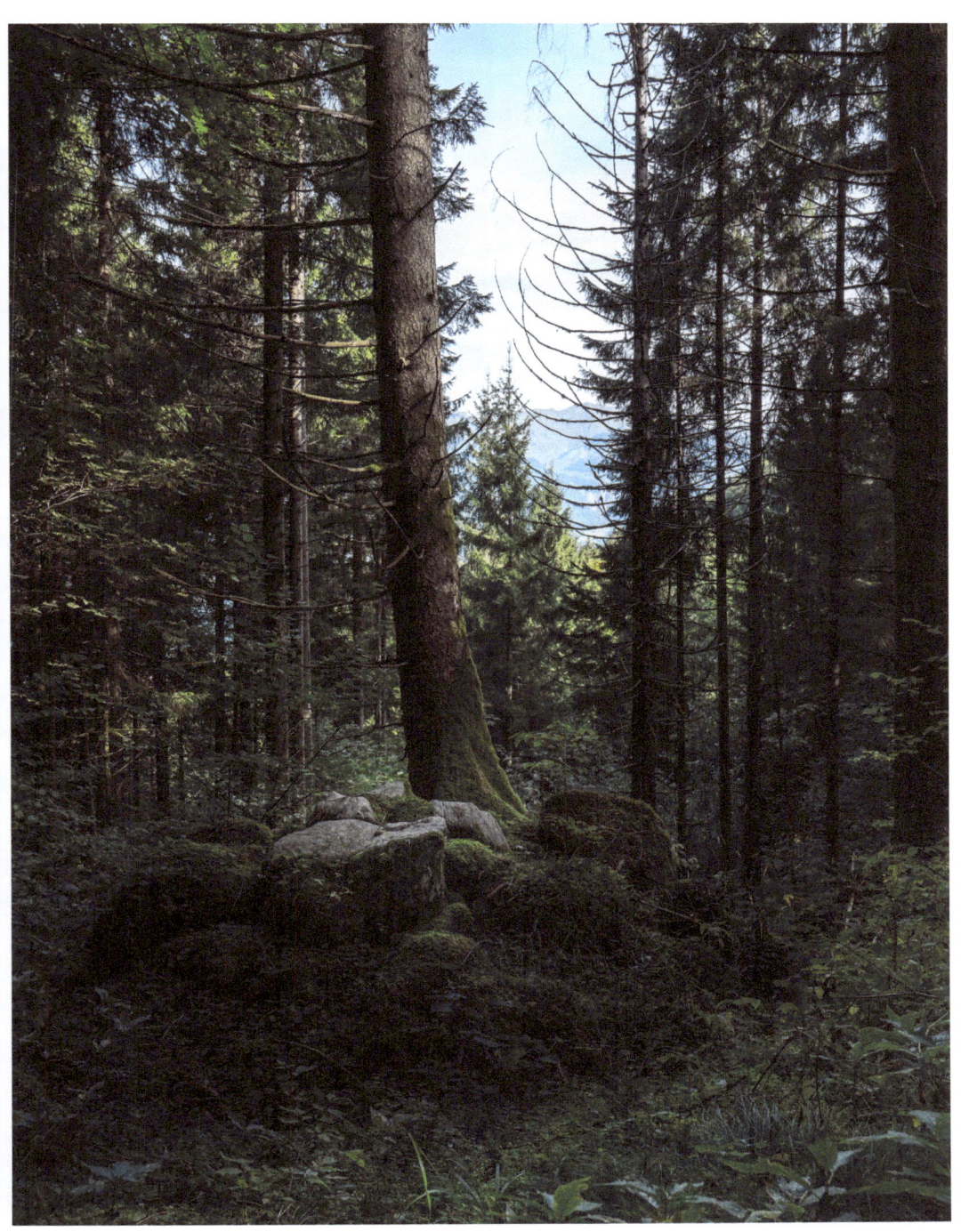

Iseltwald, Switzerland

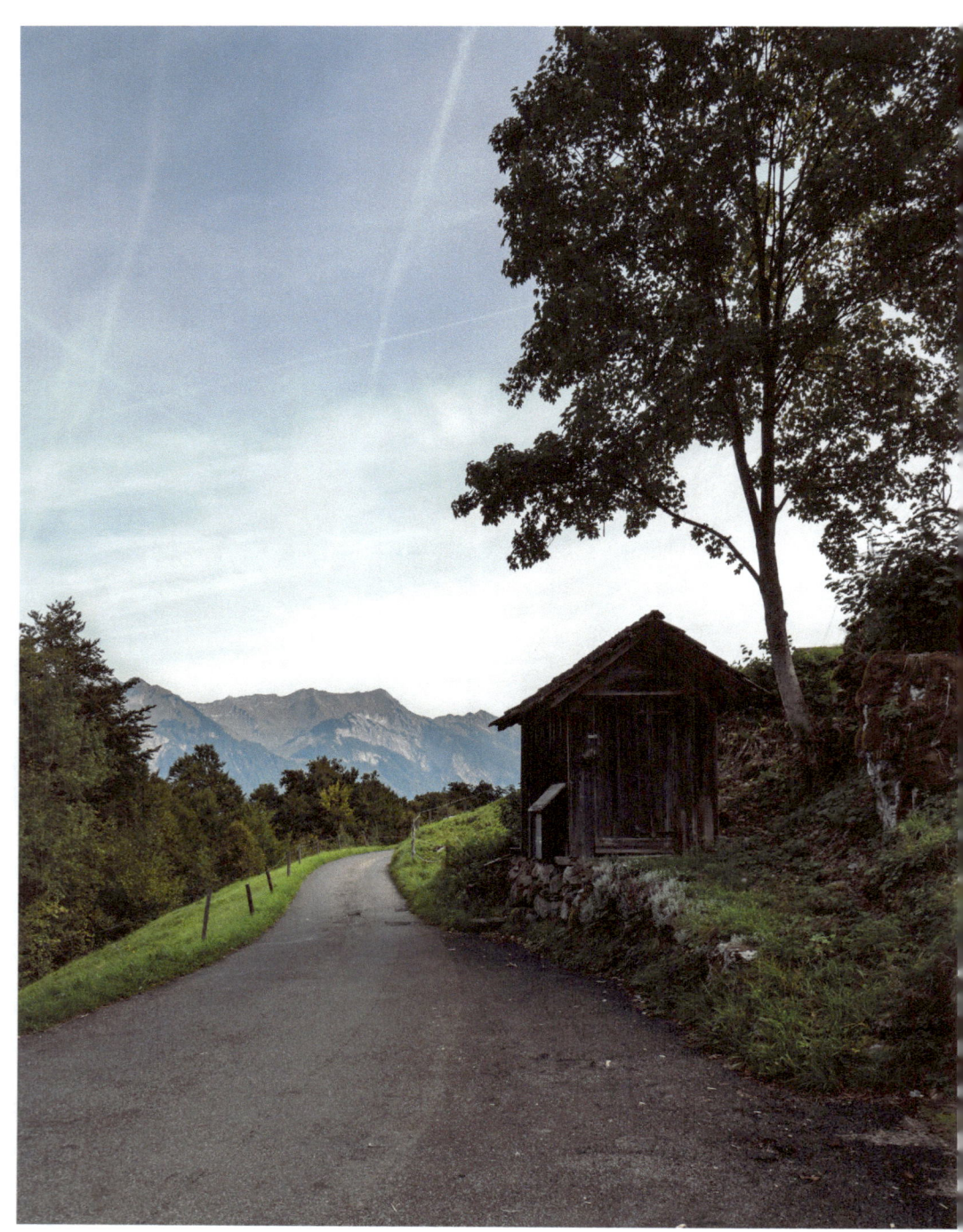

Iseltwald, Switzerland

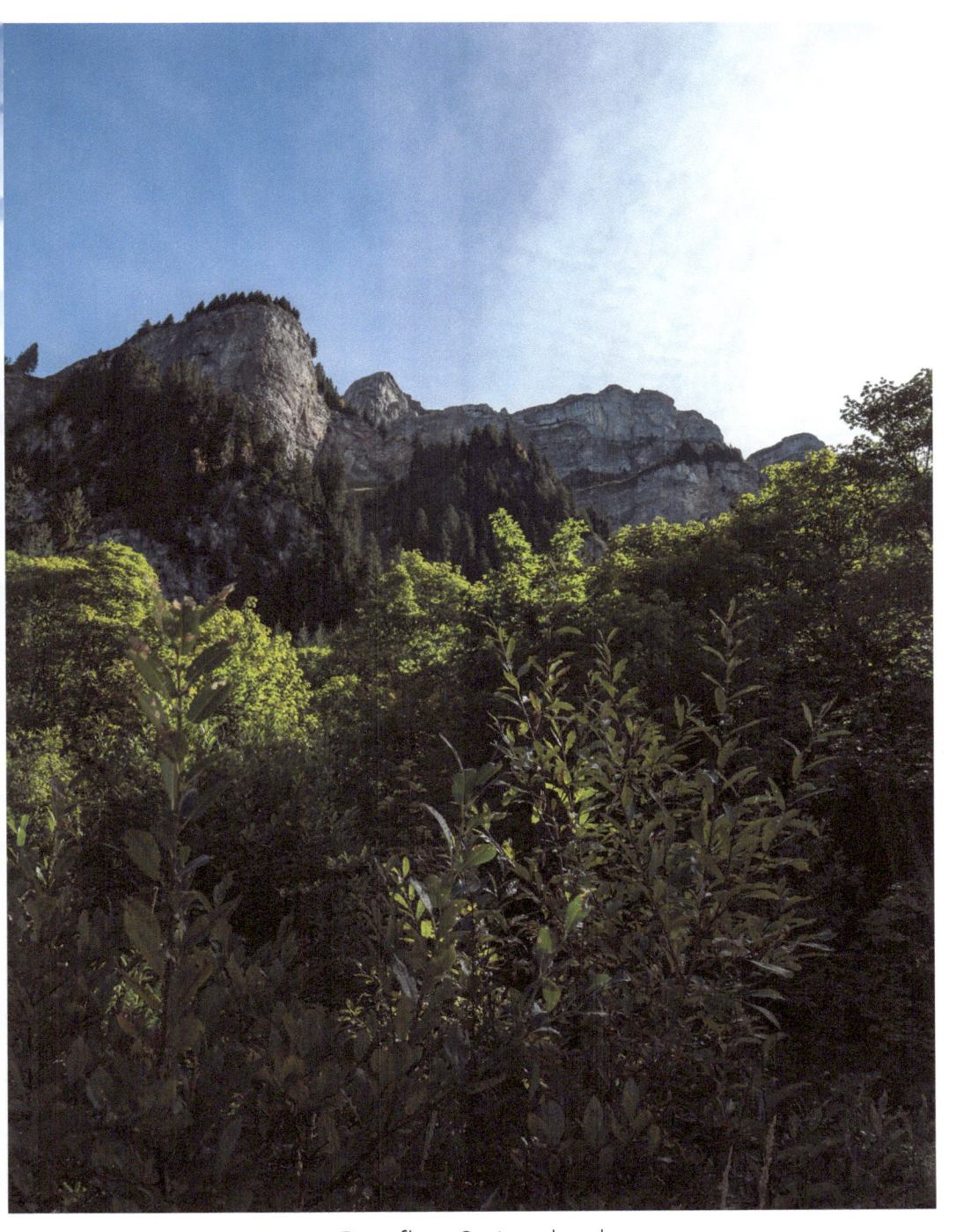

Roteflue, Switzerland

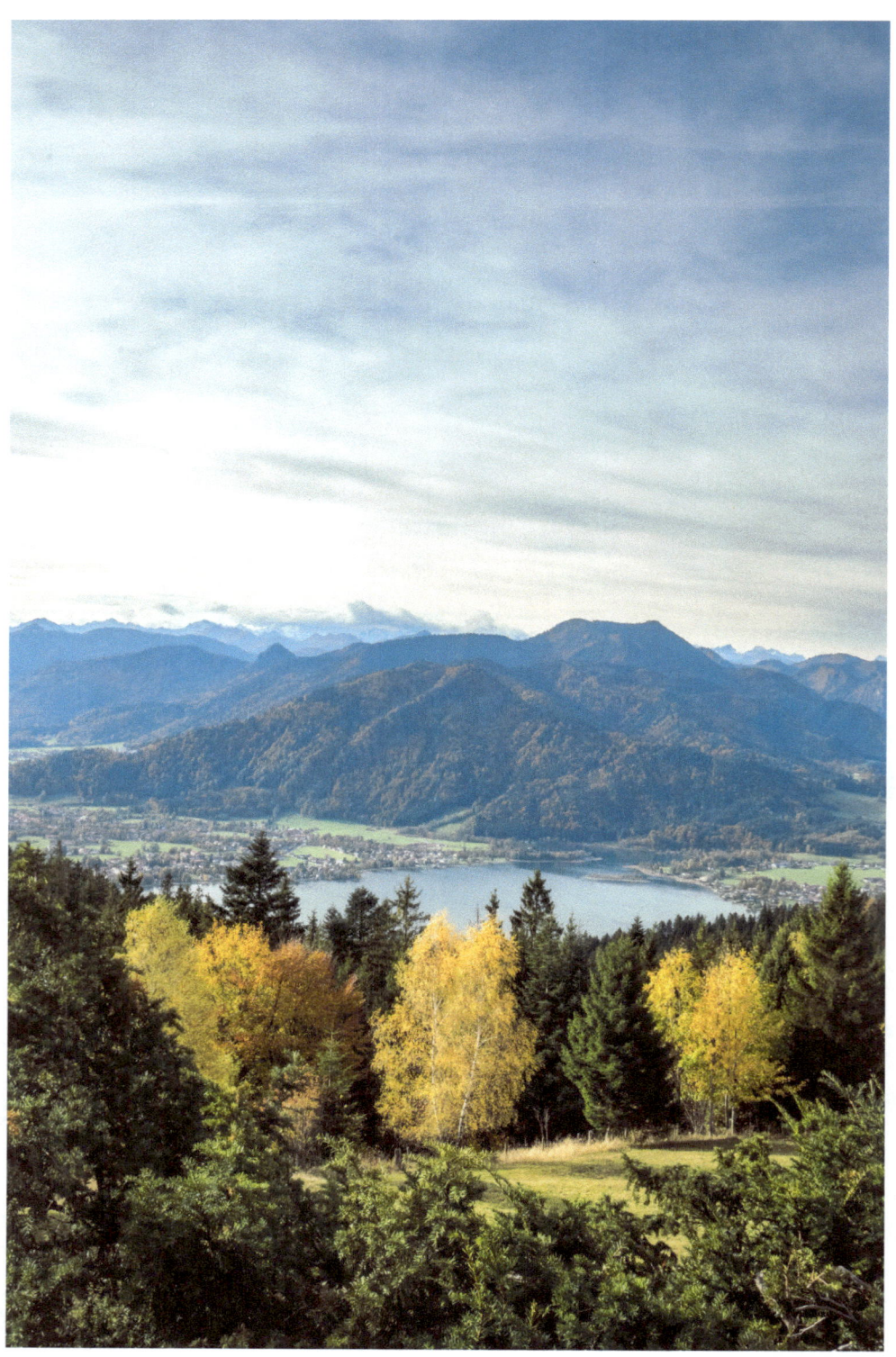

Tegernsee, Germany

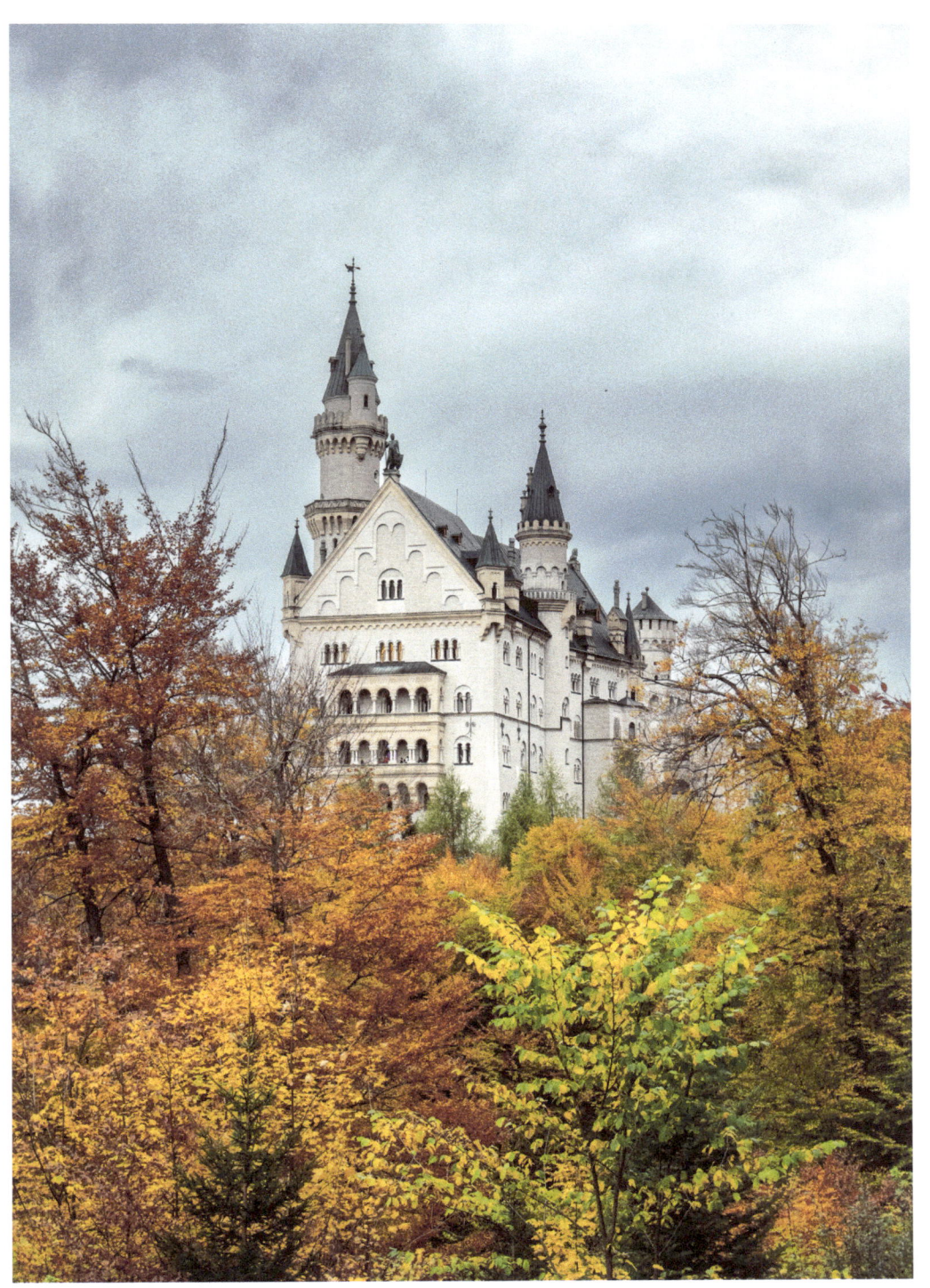

Neuschwanstein Castle, Germany

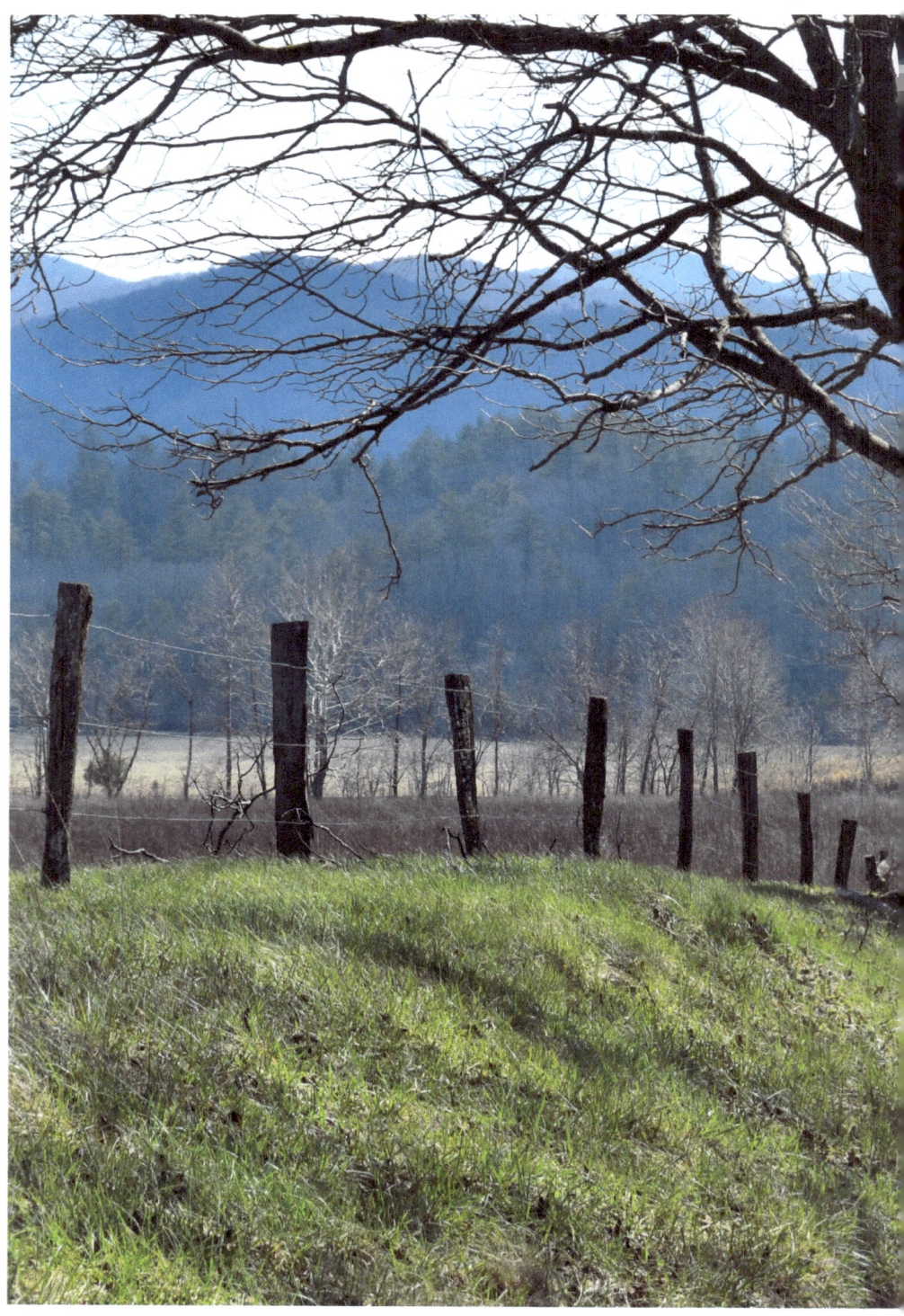

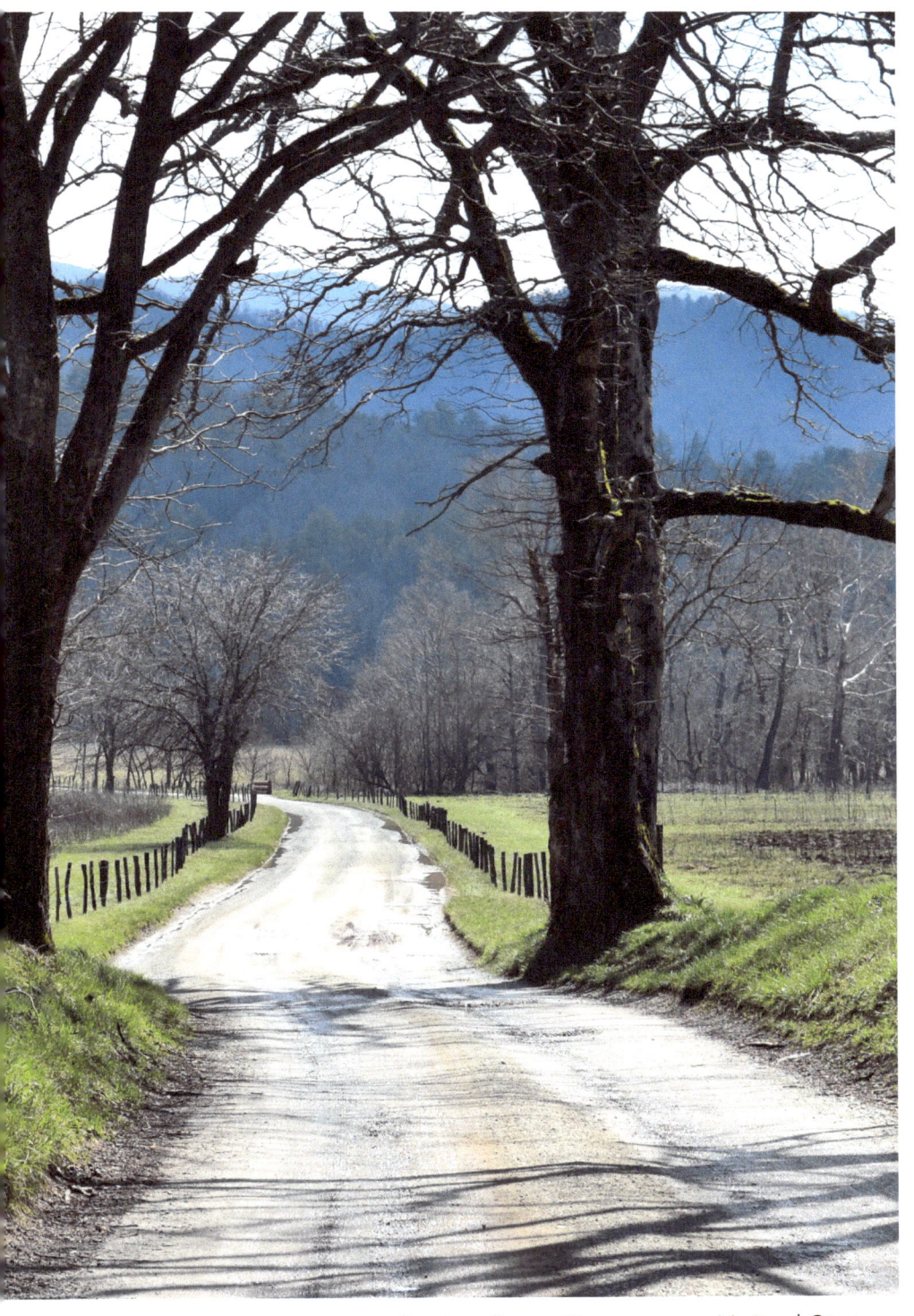
Cades Cove, Tennessee, United States

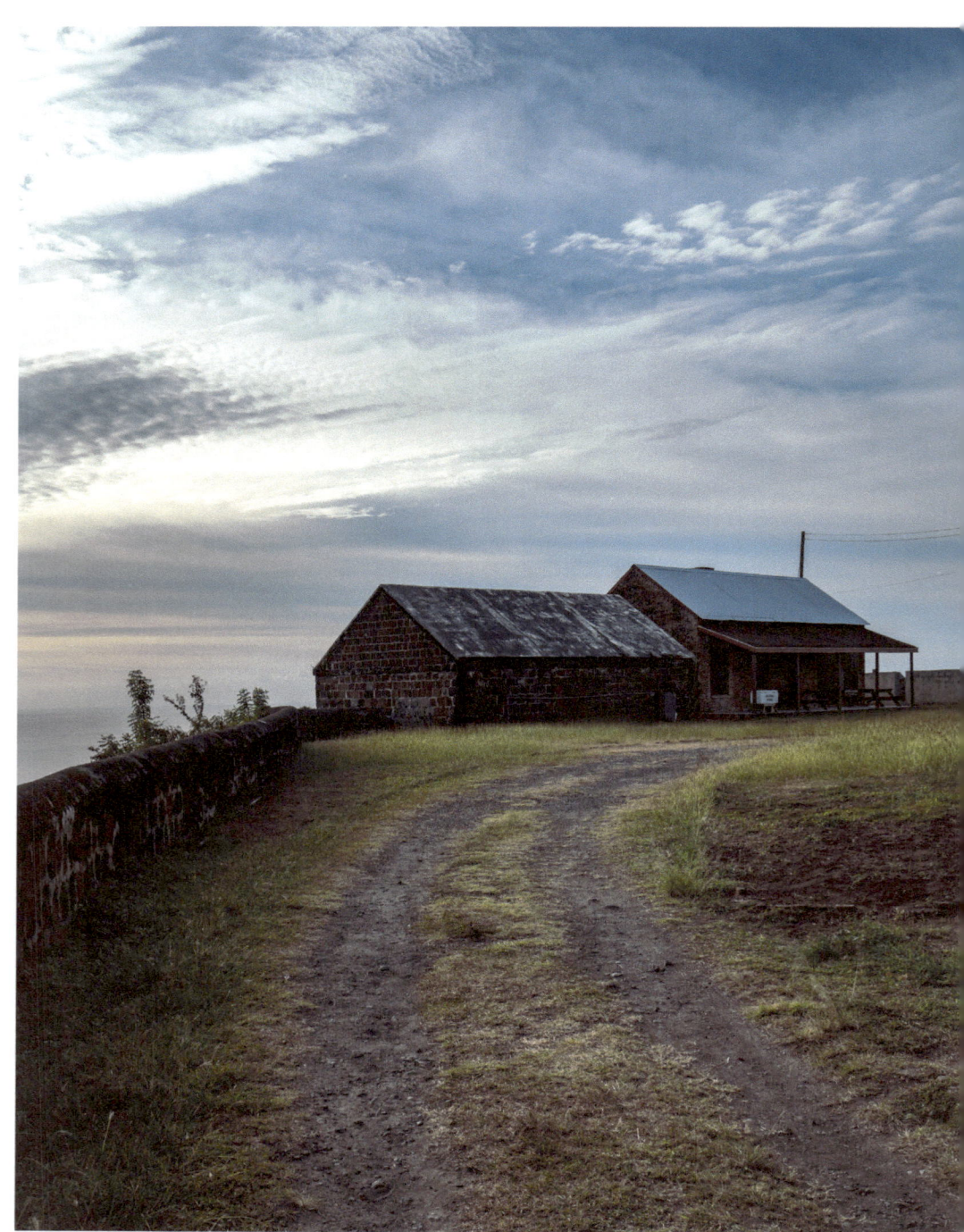

Fort Charlotte, Saint Vincent

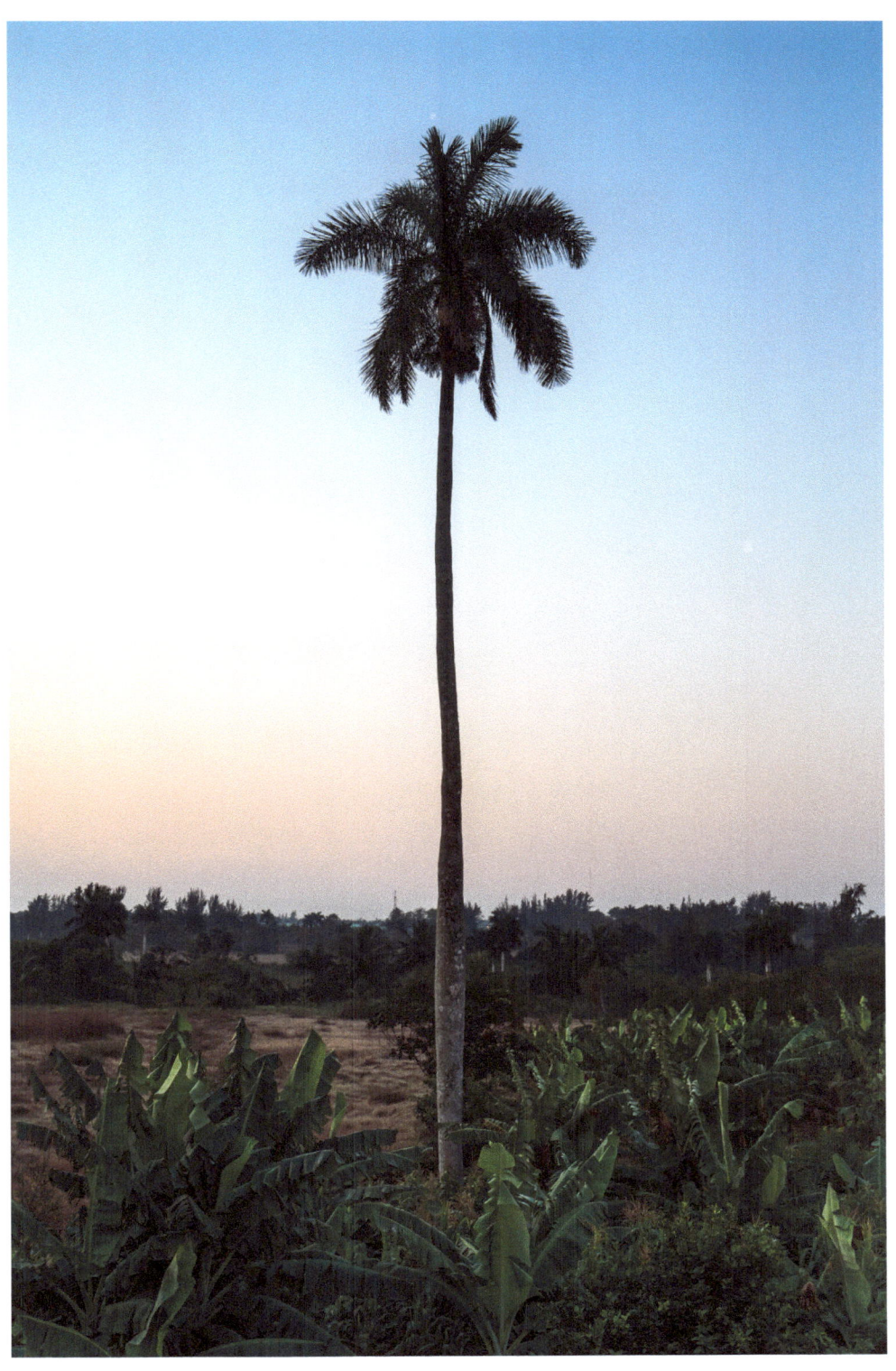

Alamar, La Habana, Cuba

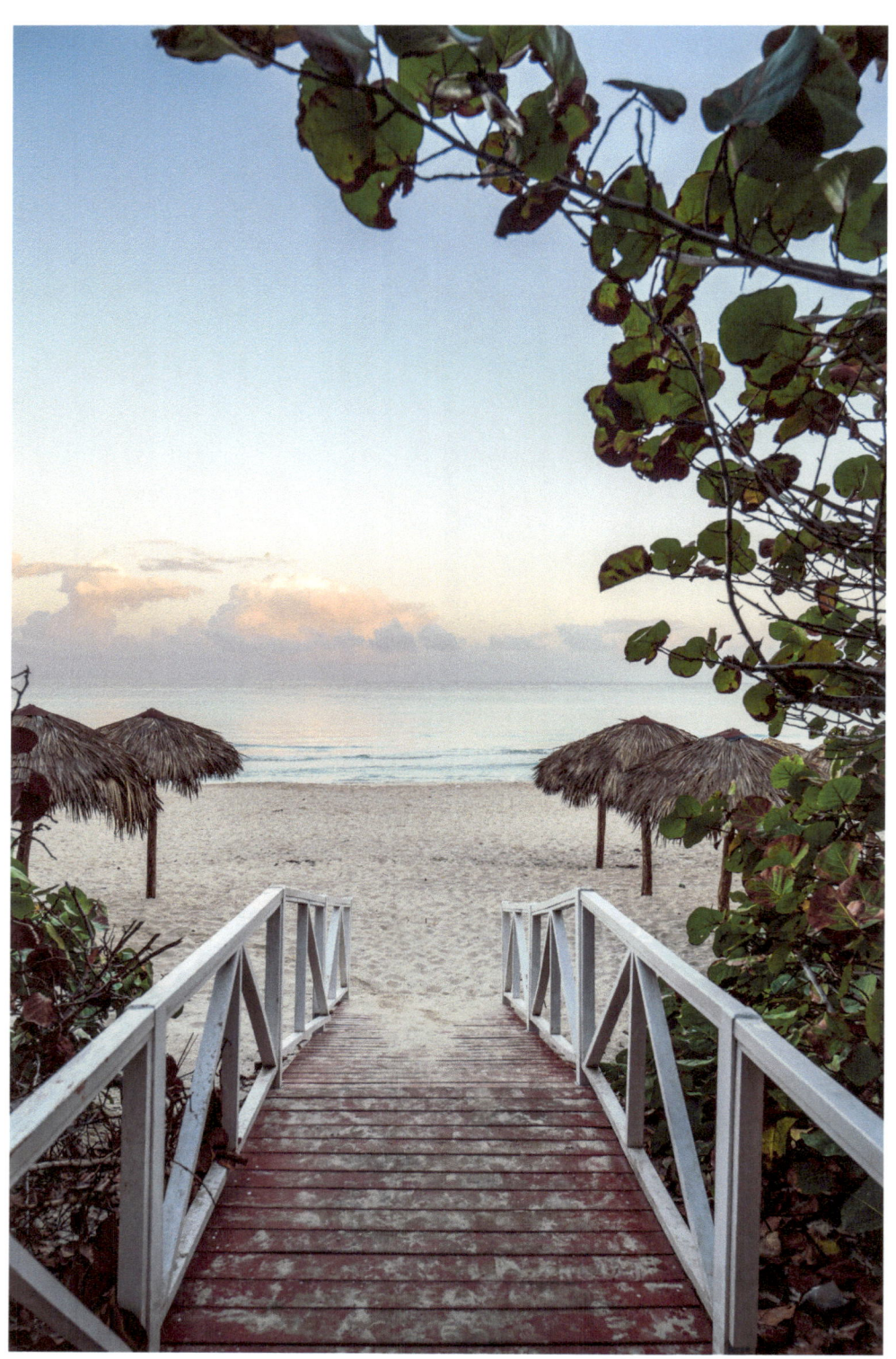

Playa Varadero, Matanzas, Cuba

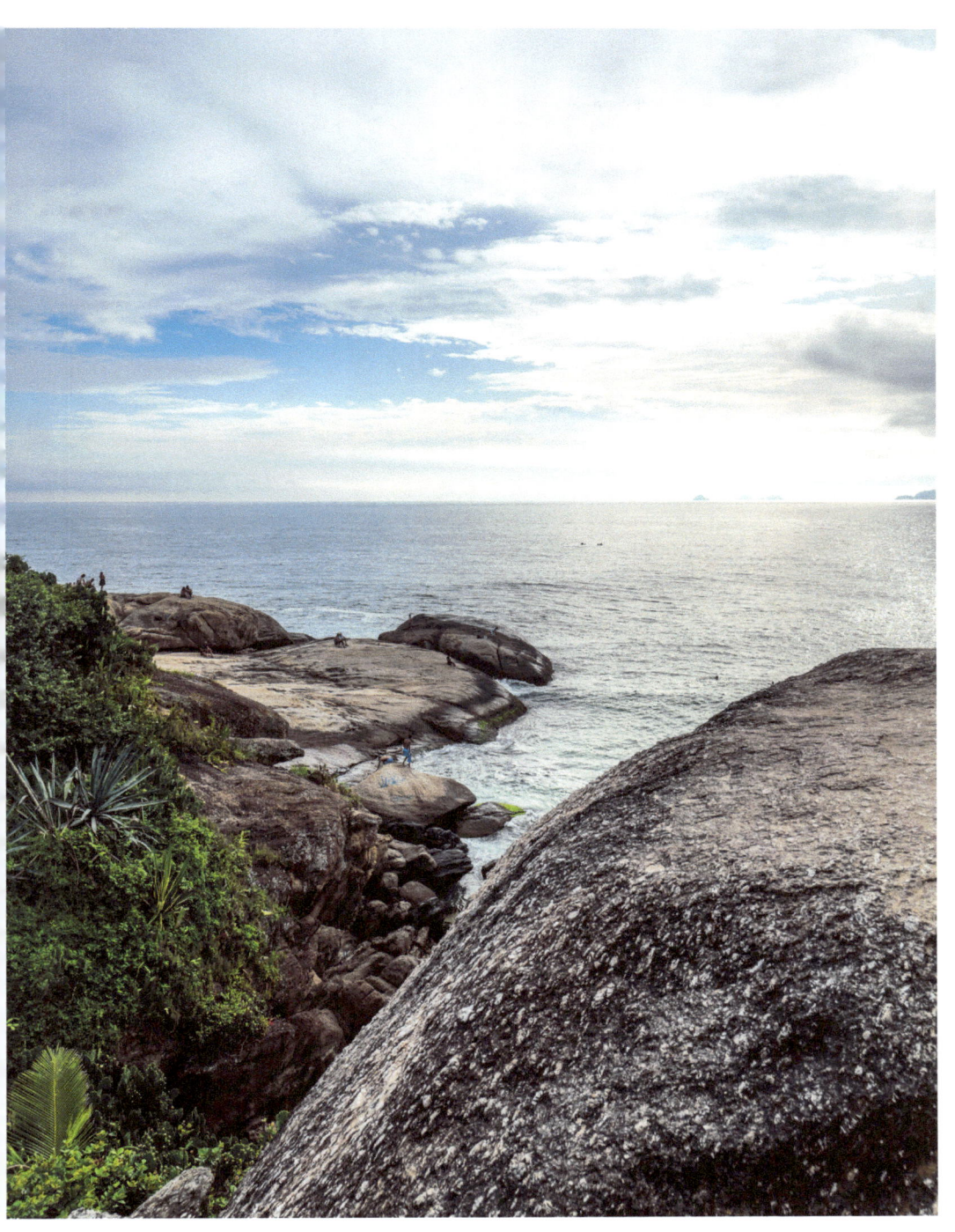

Pedra do Arpoador, Rio De Janeiro, Brasil

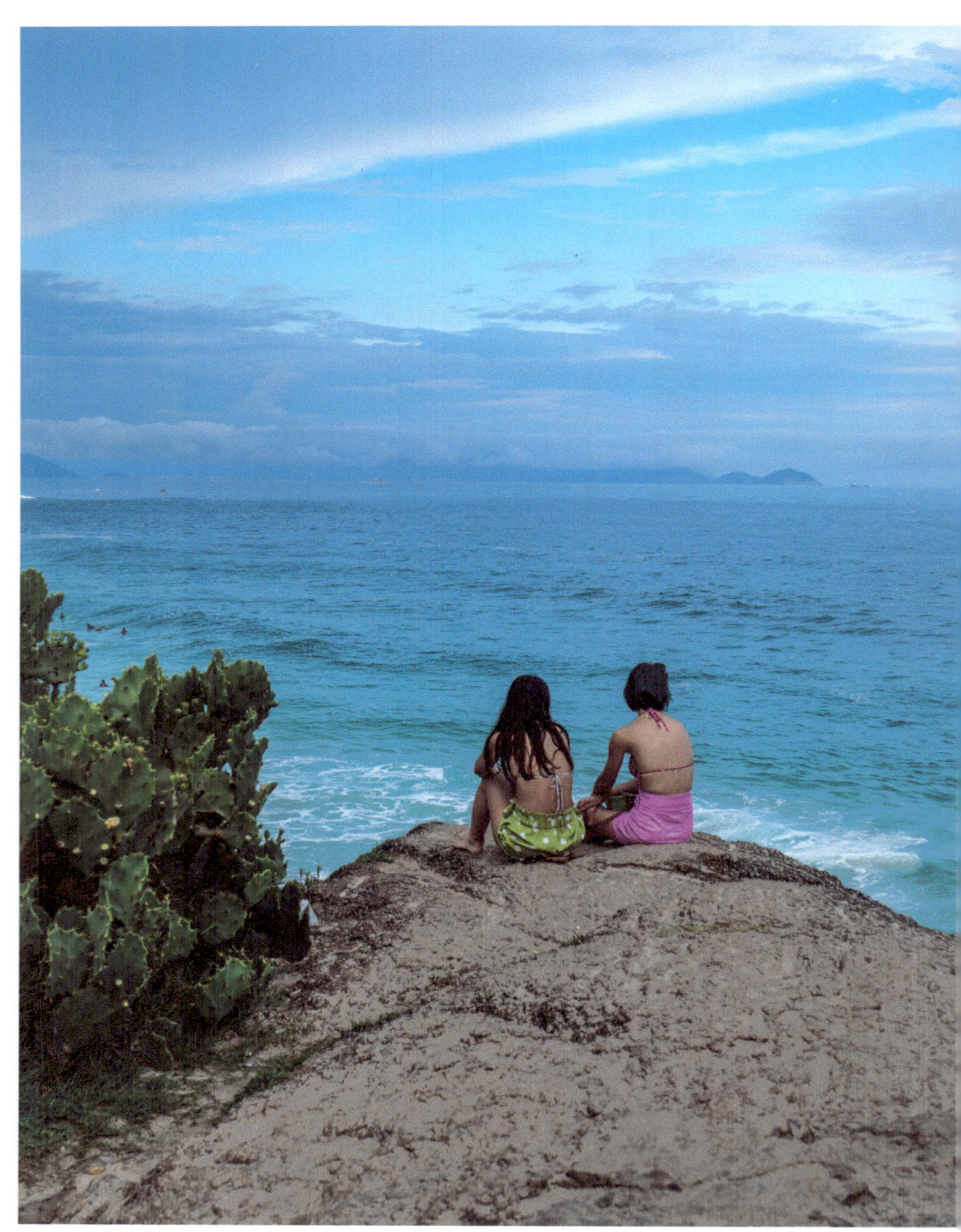

Pedra do Arpoador, Rio De Janeiro, Brasil

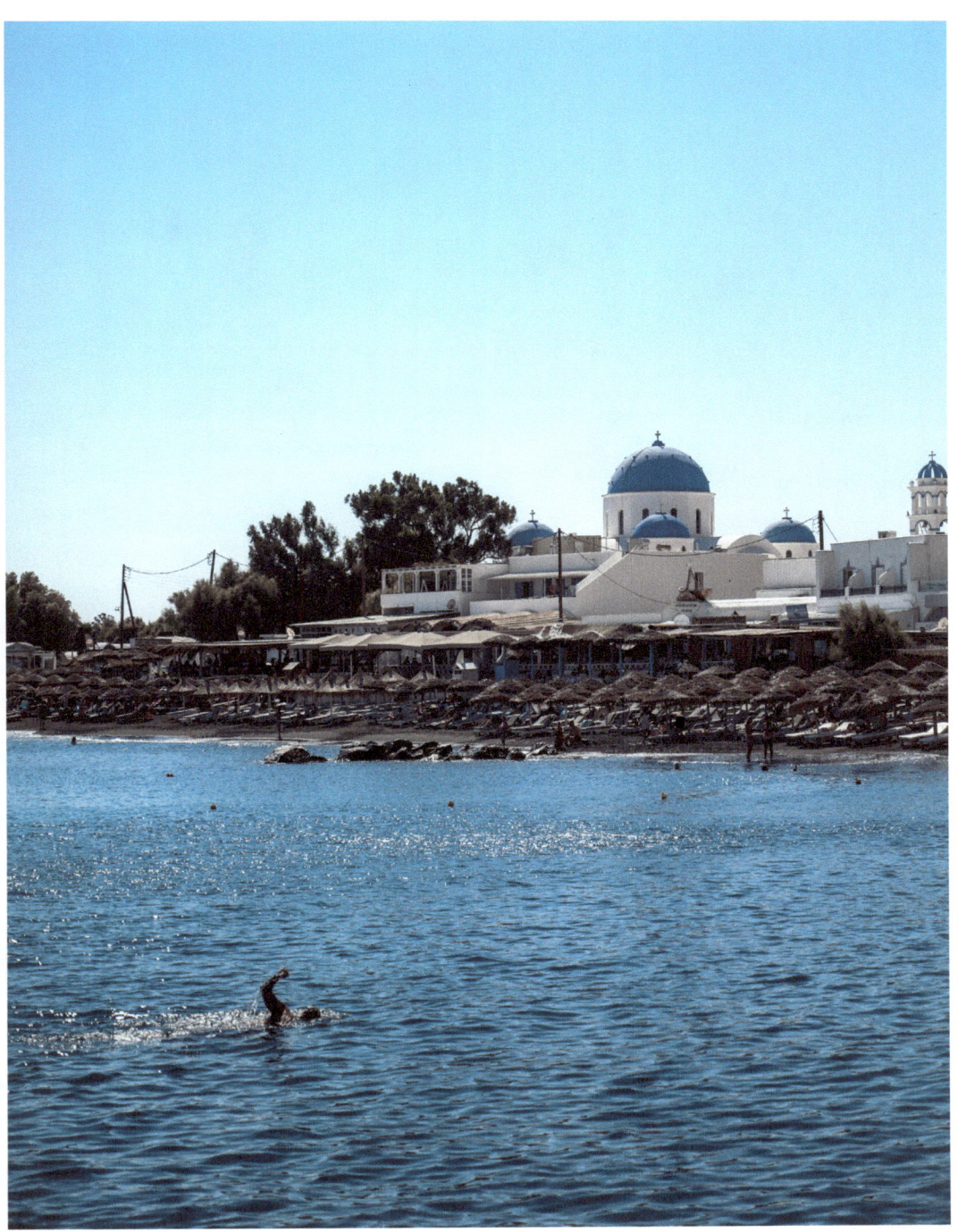

Paralia Perissa, Santorini, Greece

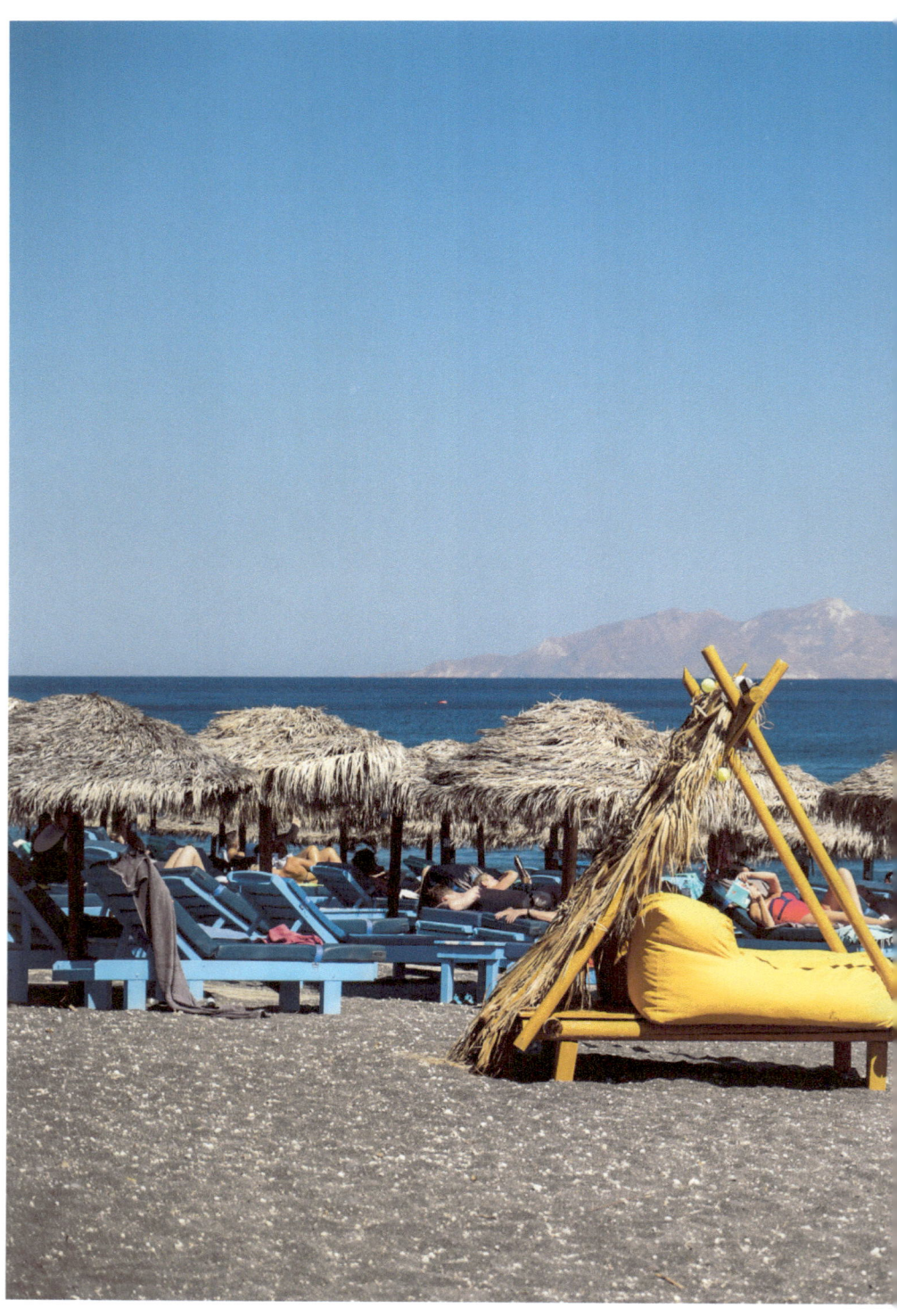

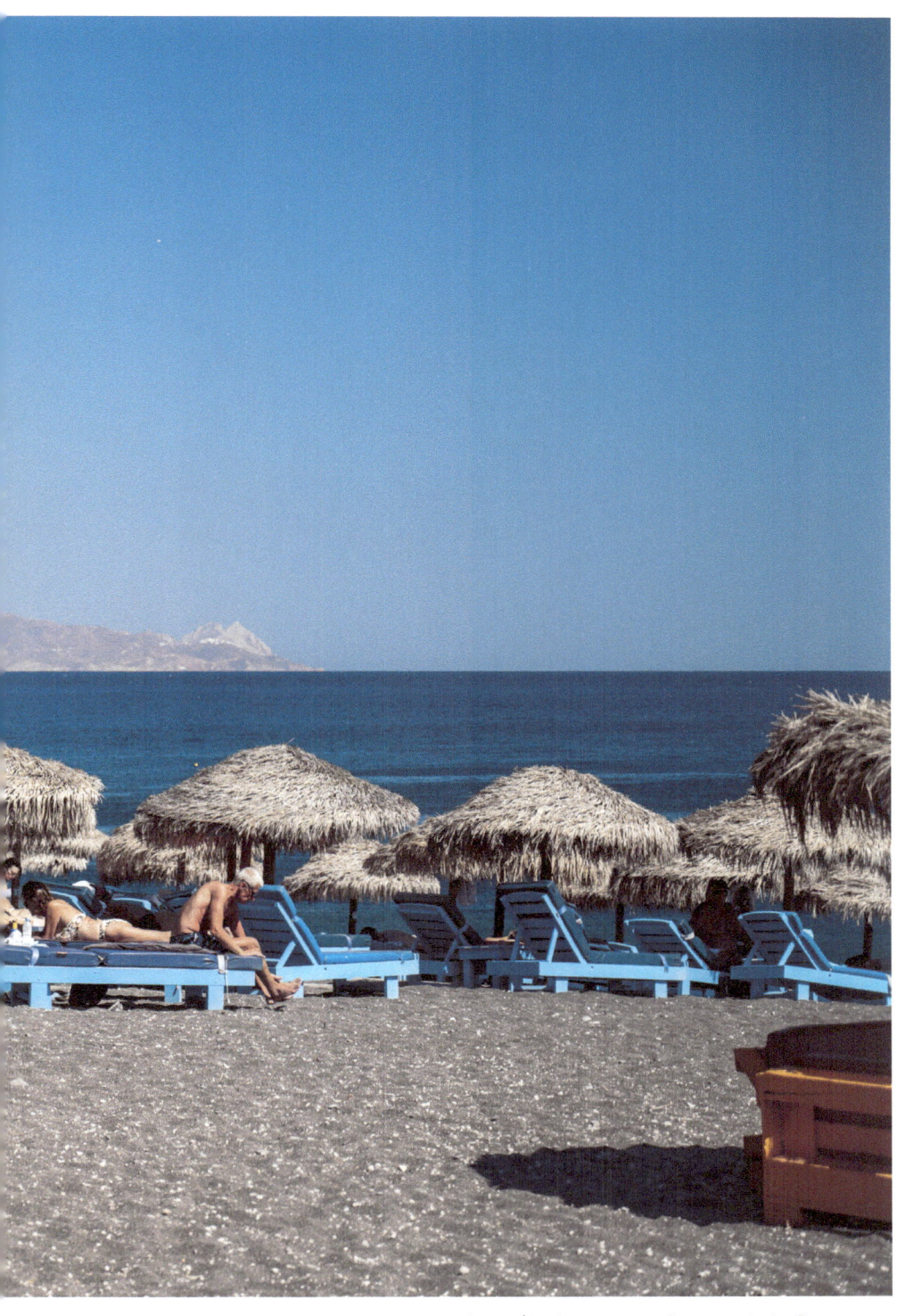

Paralia Limnes, Santorini, Greece

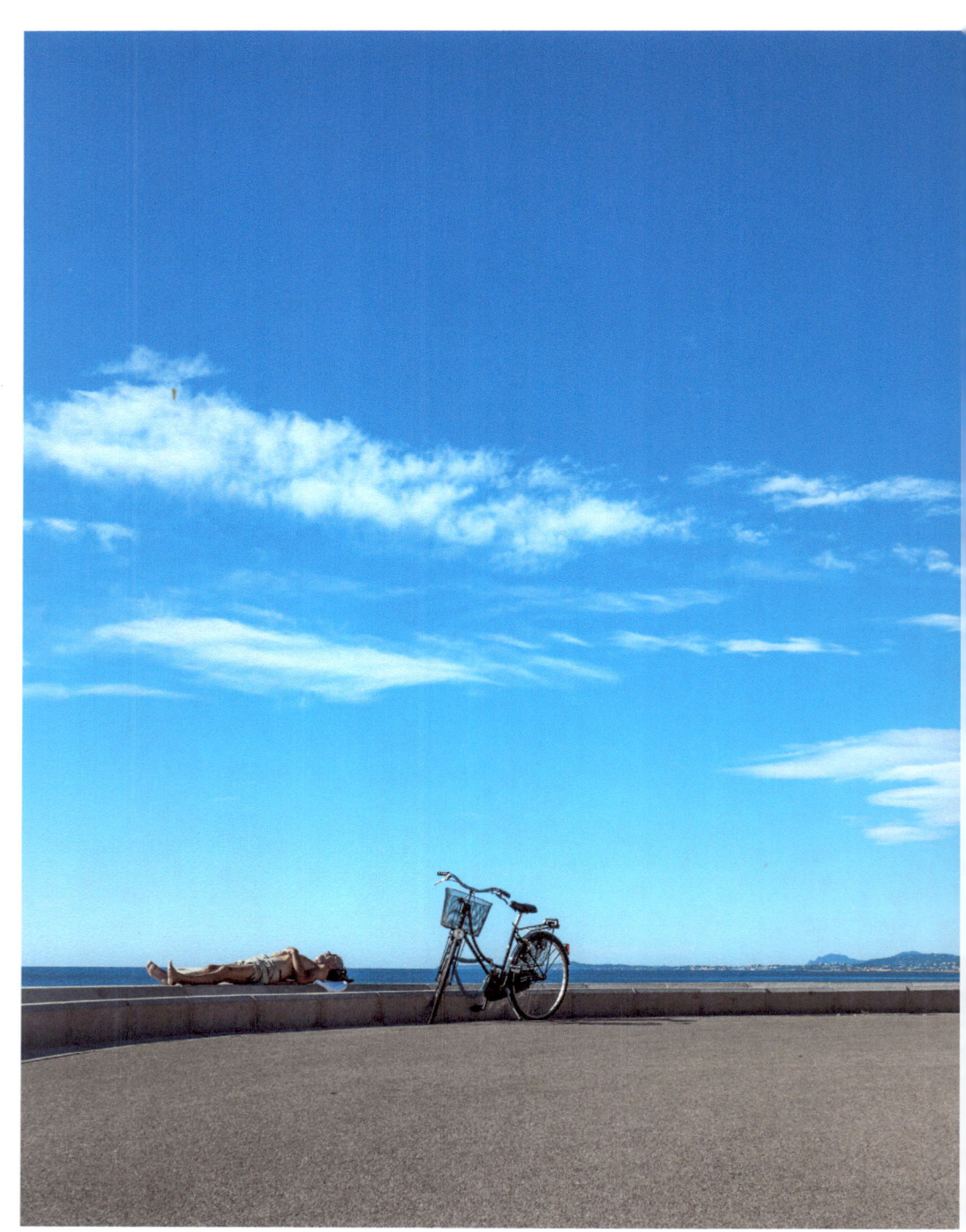

Nice, France

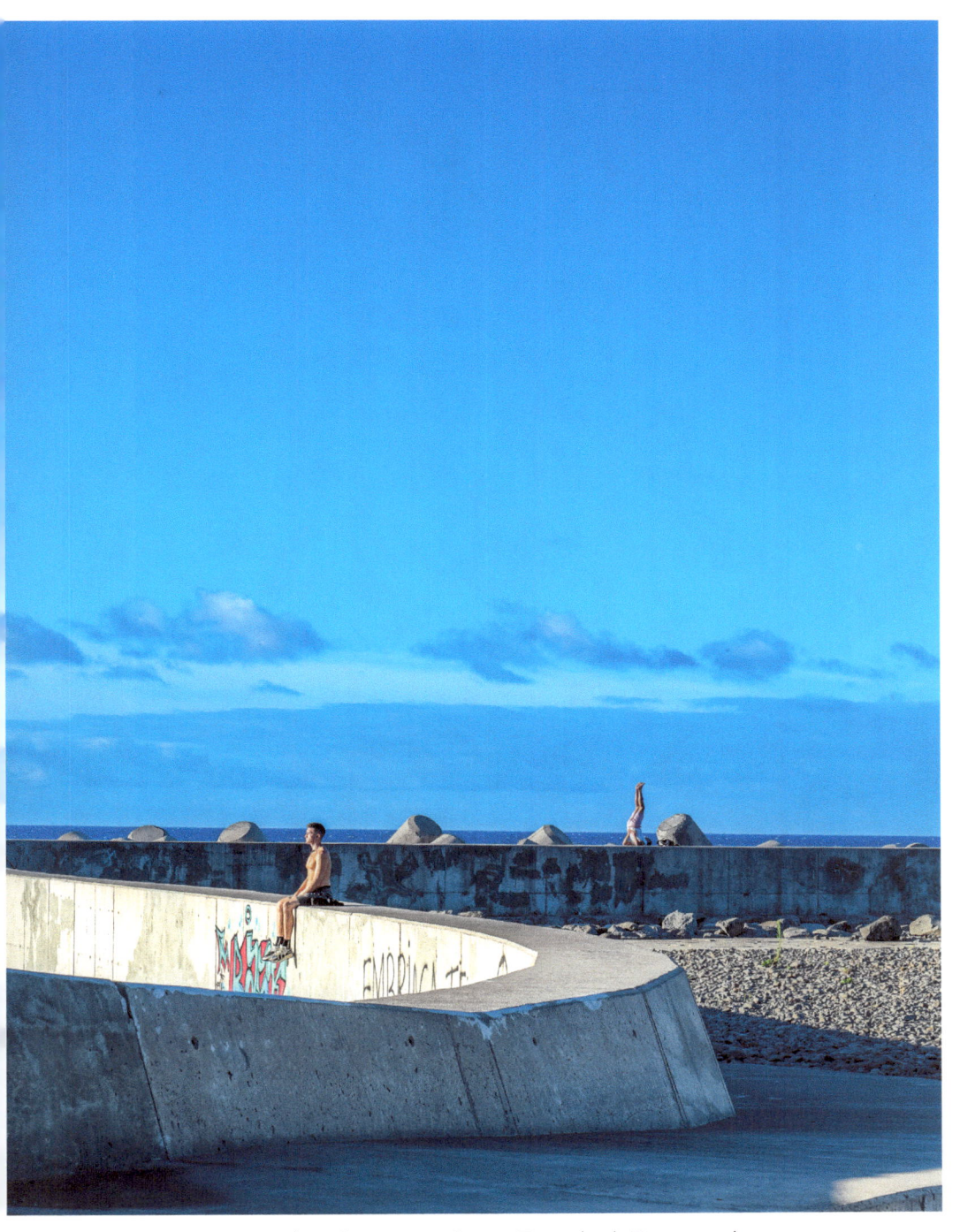

Praia do Almirante Reis, Funchal, Portugal

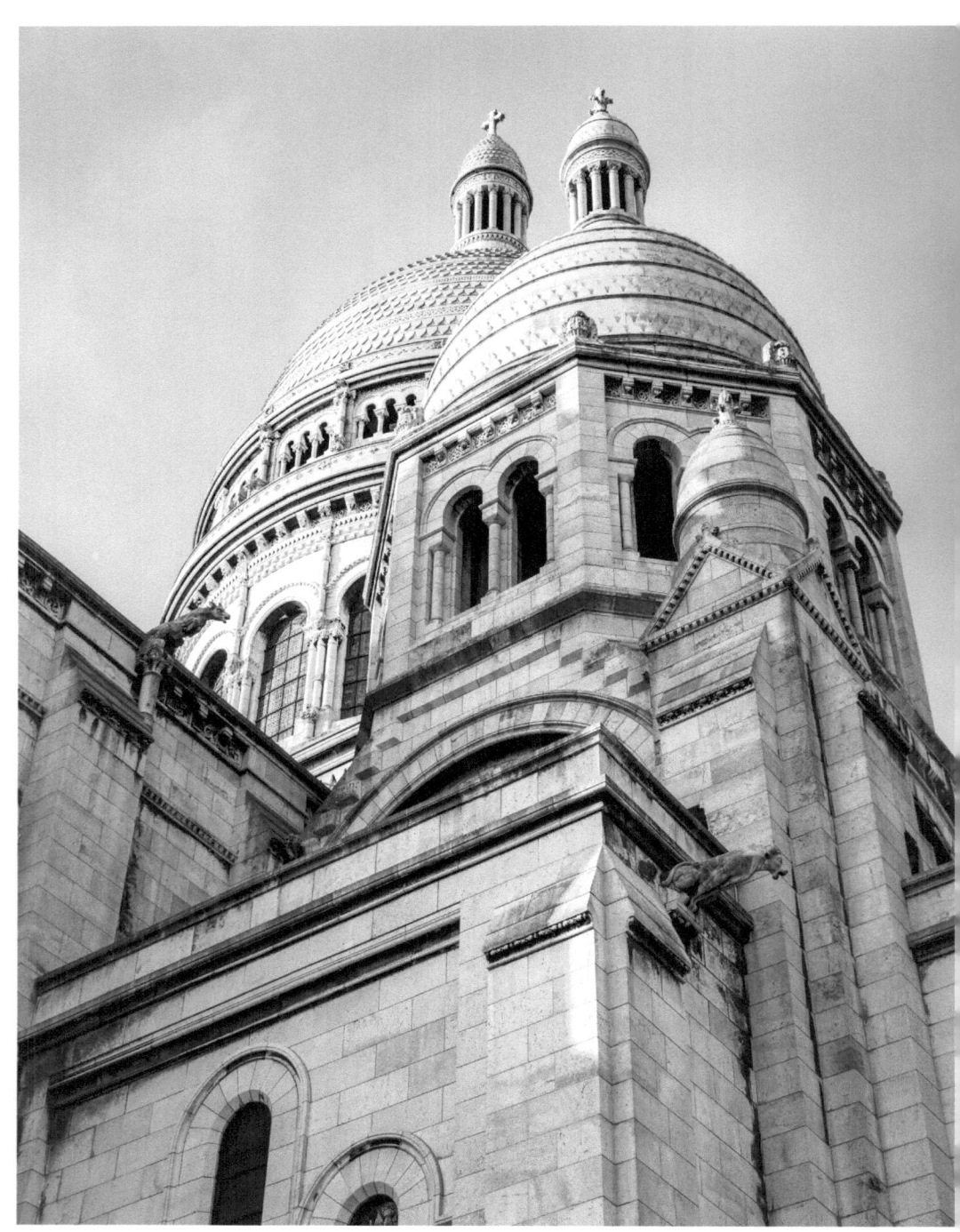
The Basilica of Sacré-Cœur de Montmartre, Paris, France

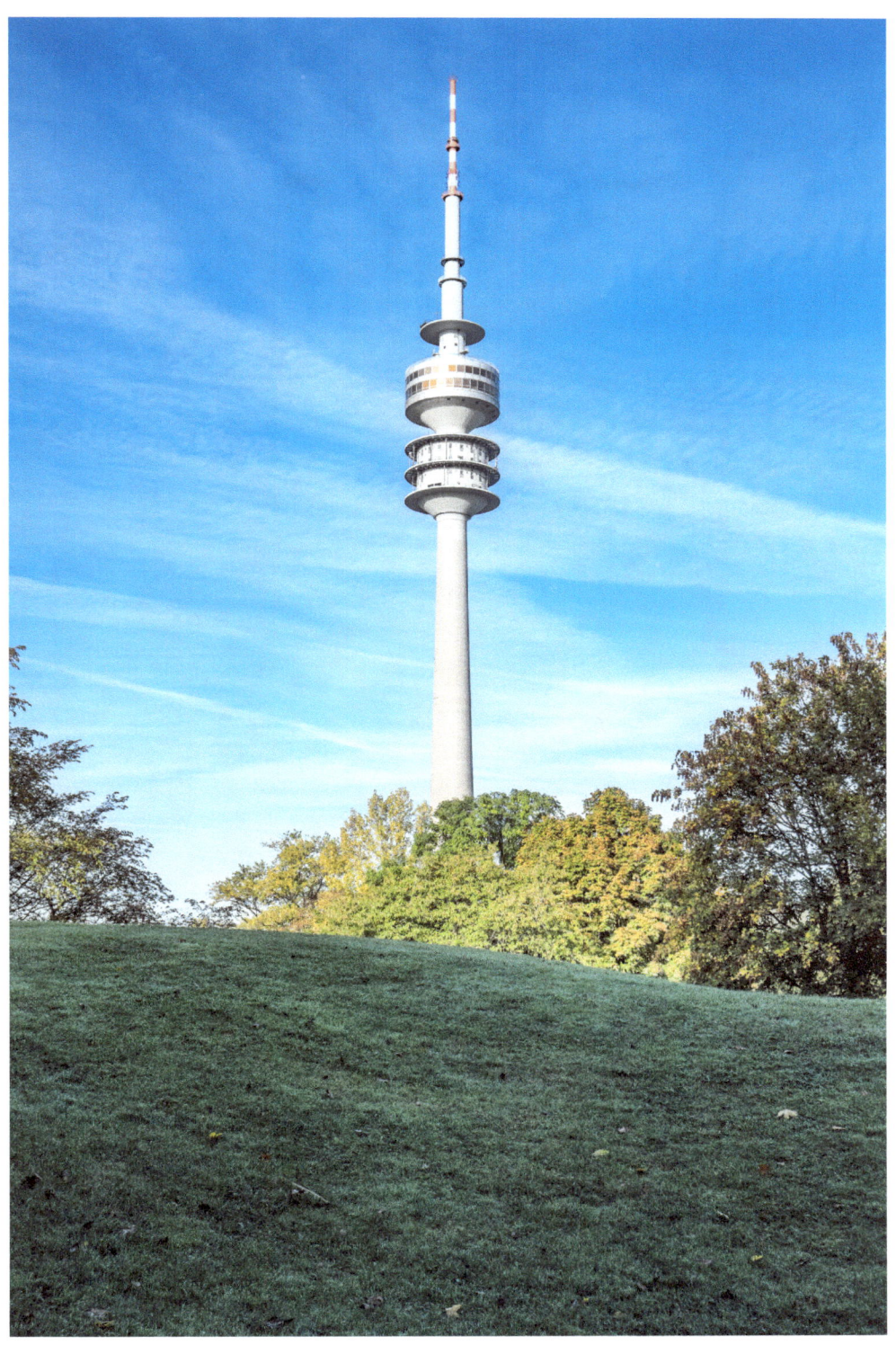

Germany

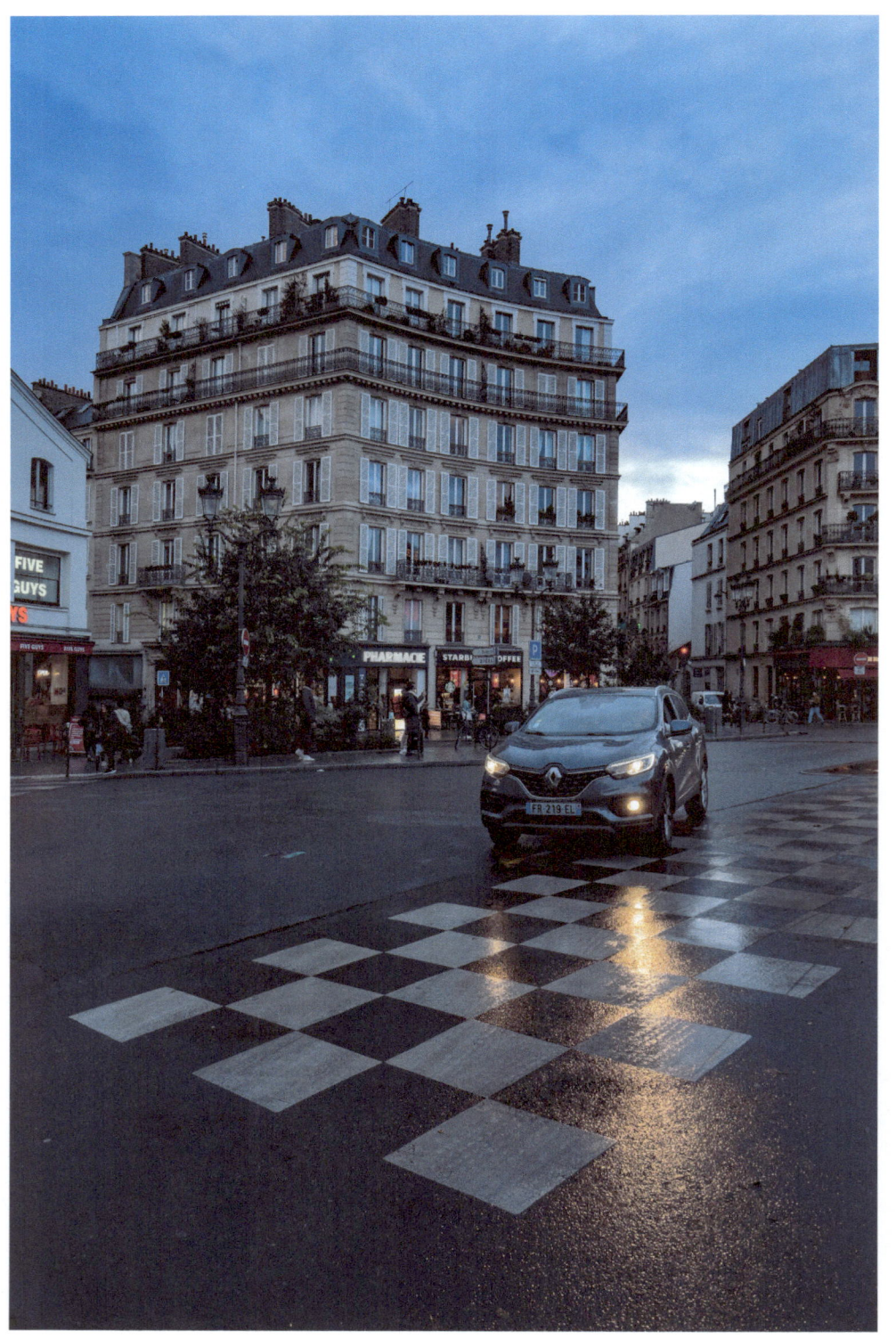

Place Blanche, Paris, France

Let me speak to you who reads because today no one listens. Perhaps tomorrow you can shout my words and be heard, perhaps once the noise vanishes.

Because music has gone from strings to steel, and sounds of birds to sounds of mills. And beauty has disappeared by man's will.

We've transformed mountains from green to gray and turned playing fields into entertainment reels. Today's children no longer play. As the world morphs into concrete walls; finding beauty only gets hard.

Preferring the evening daze over a morning haze, and lost in the buzz of neon lights, we've darkened our days to light up the nights.

We've turned our seas from blue to black and dumped our worries without looking back. Soon we'll drown in the search for beauty that is no longer found.

Thankfully, we still have places to hide, those of us looking for nature and nothing more — An escape from the toxic rush. I invite you to explore; go and seek the beauty that this world beholds.

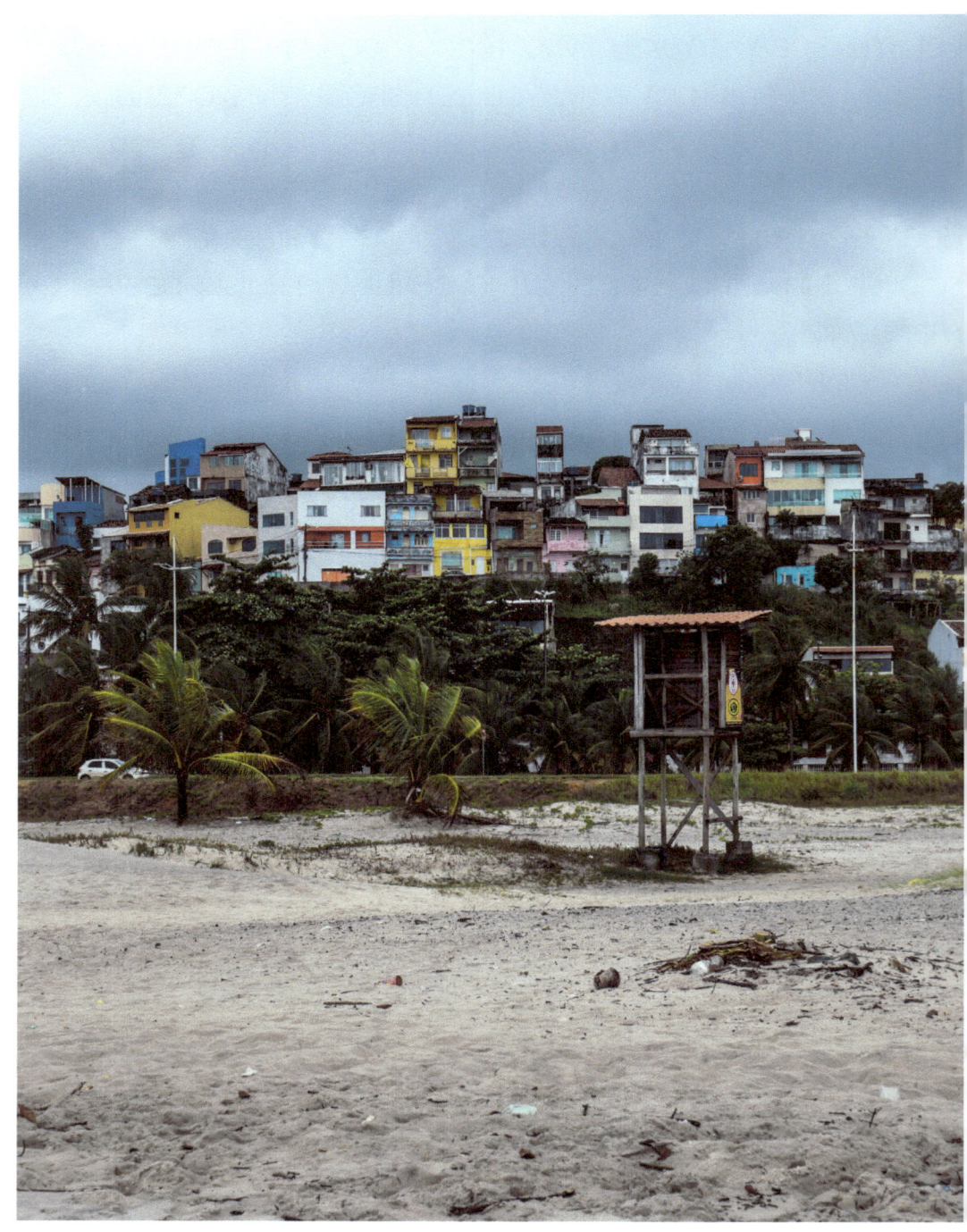

Praia da Avenida, Ilhéus, Brasil

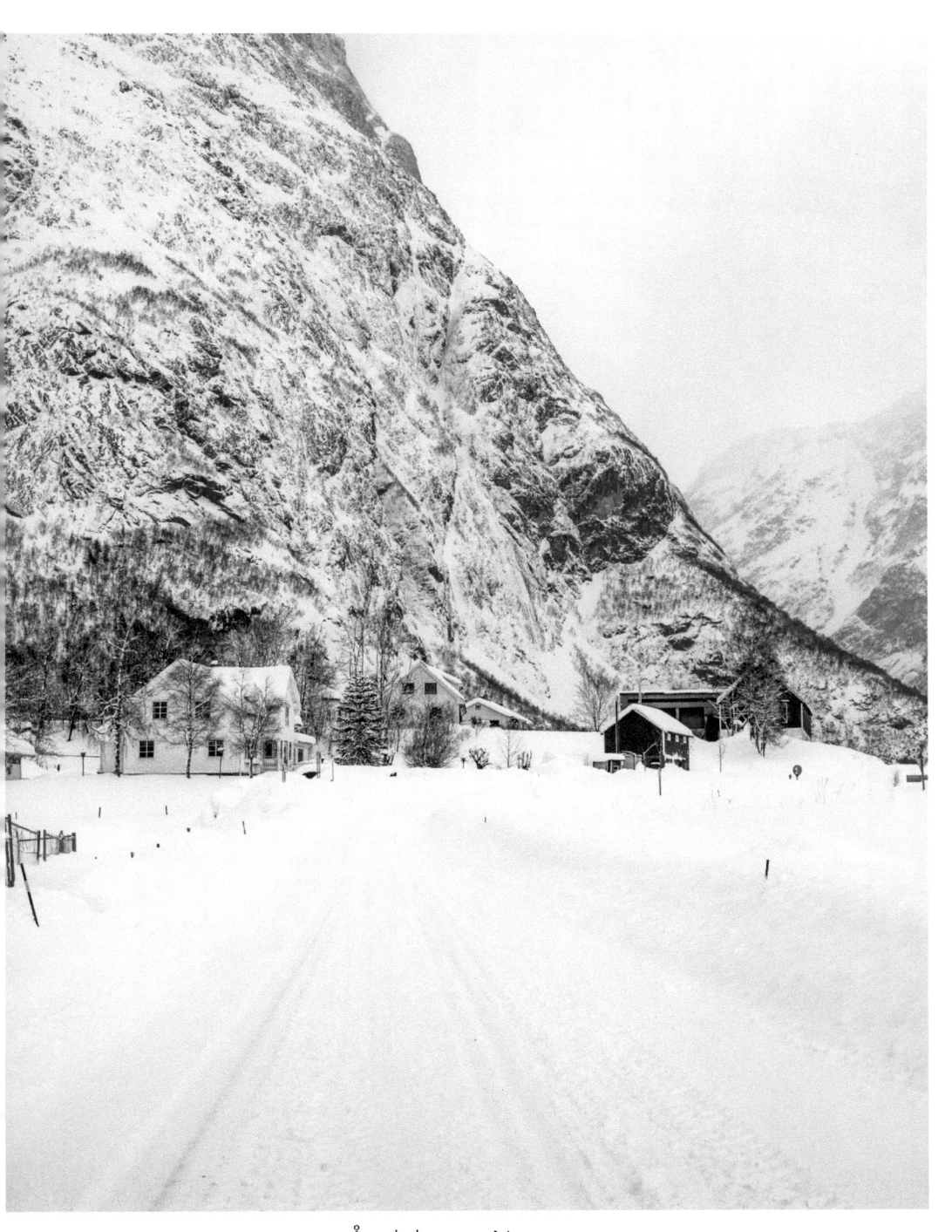

Åndalsnes, Norway

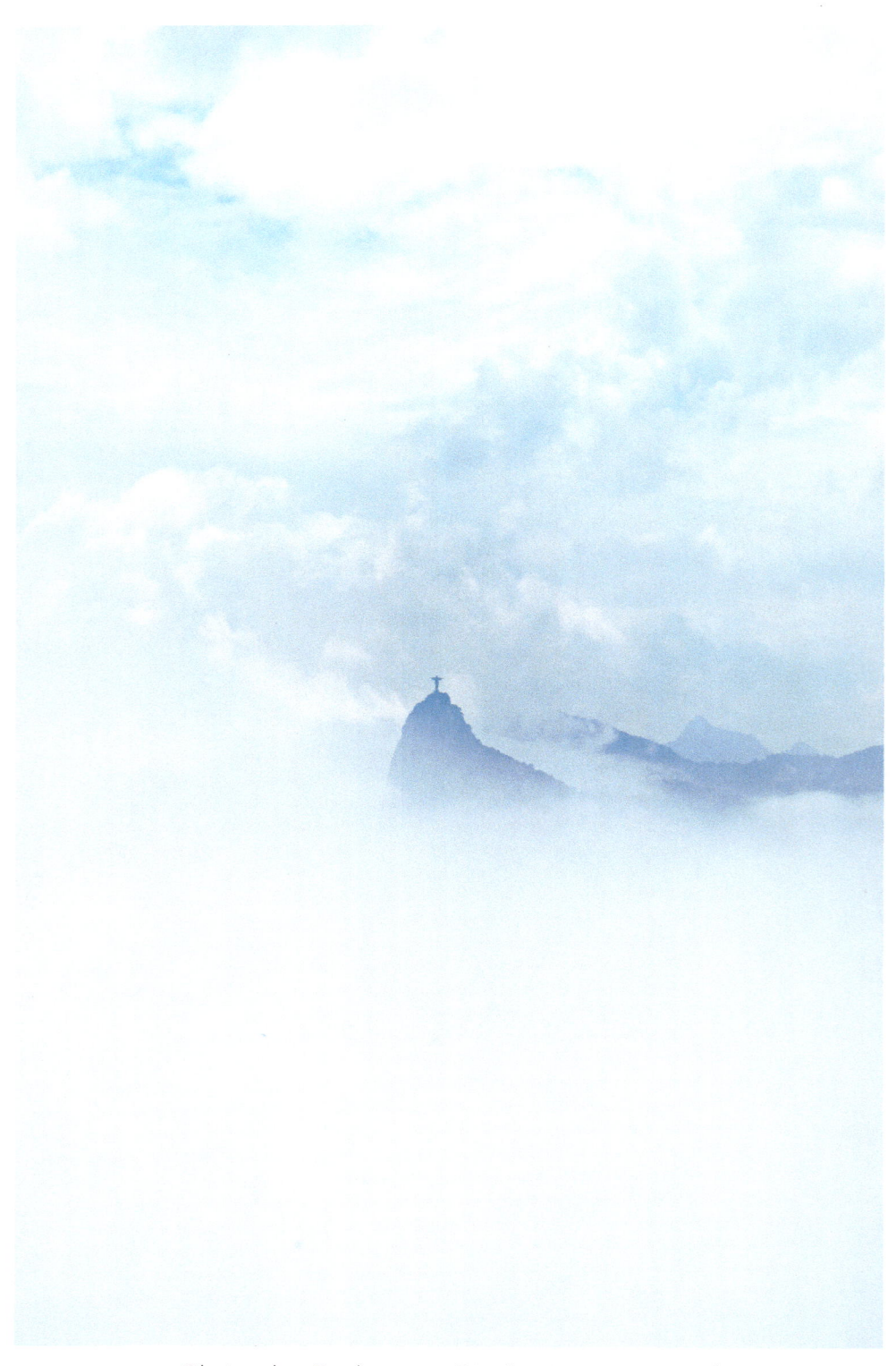

Christ the Redeemer, Rio De Janeiro, Brasil

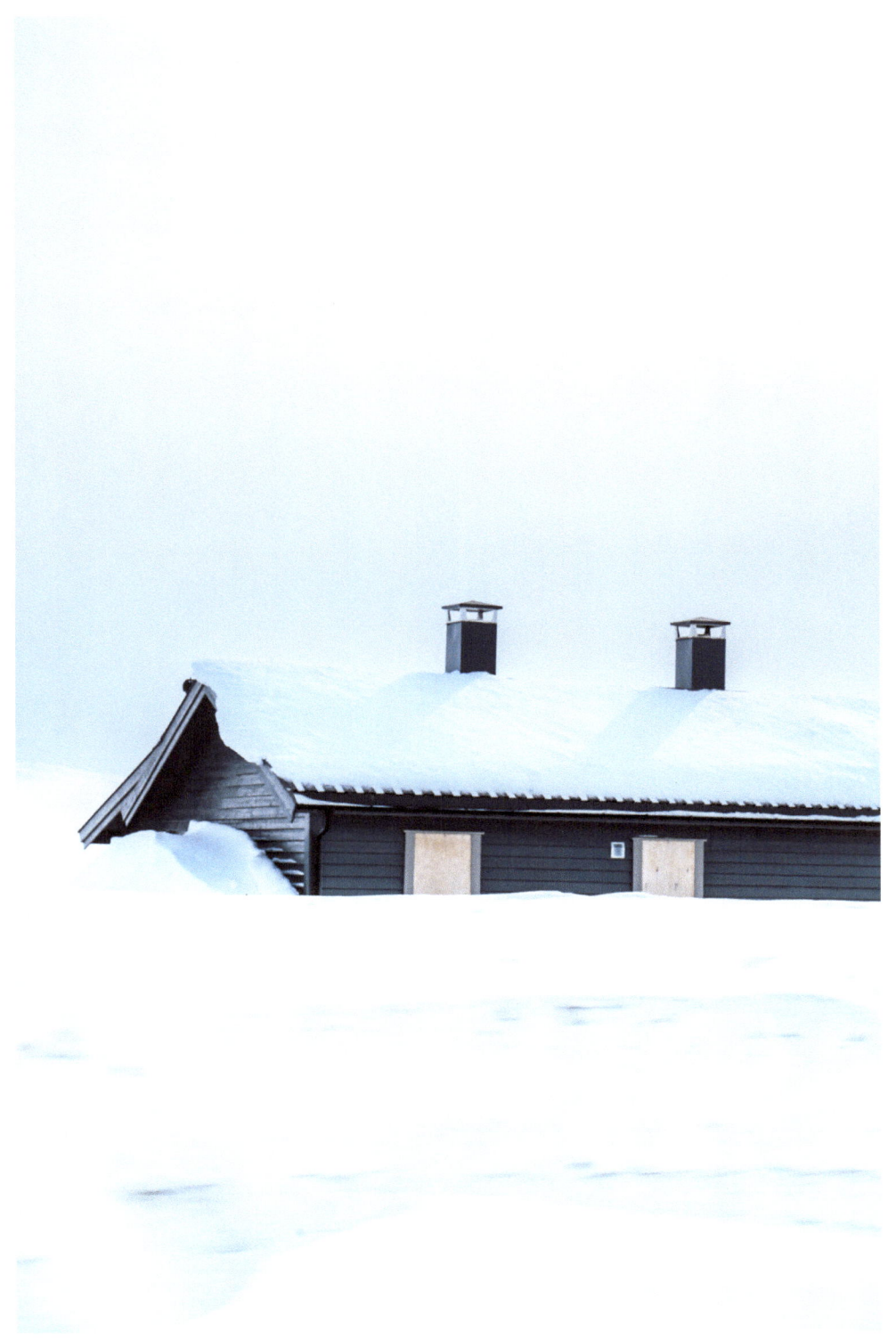

Geilo, Norway

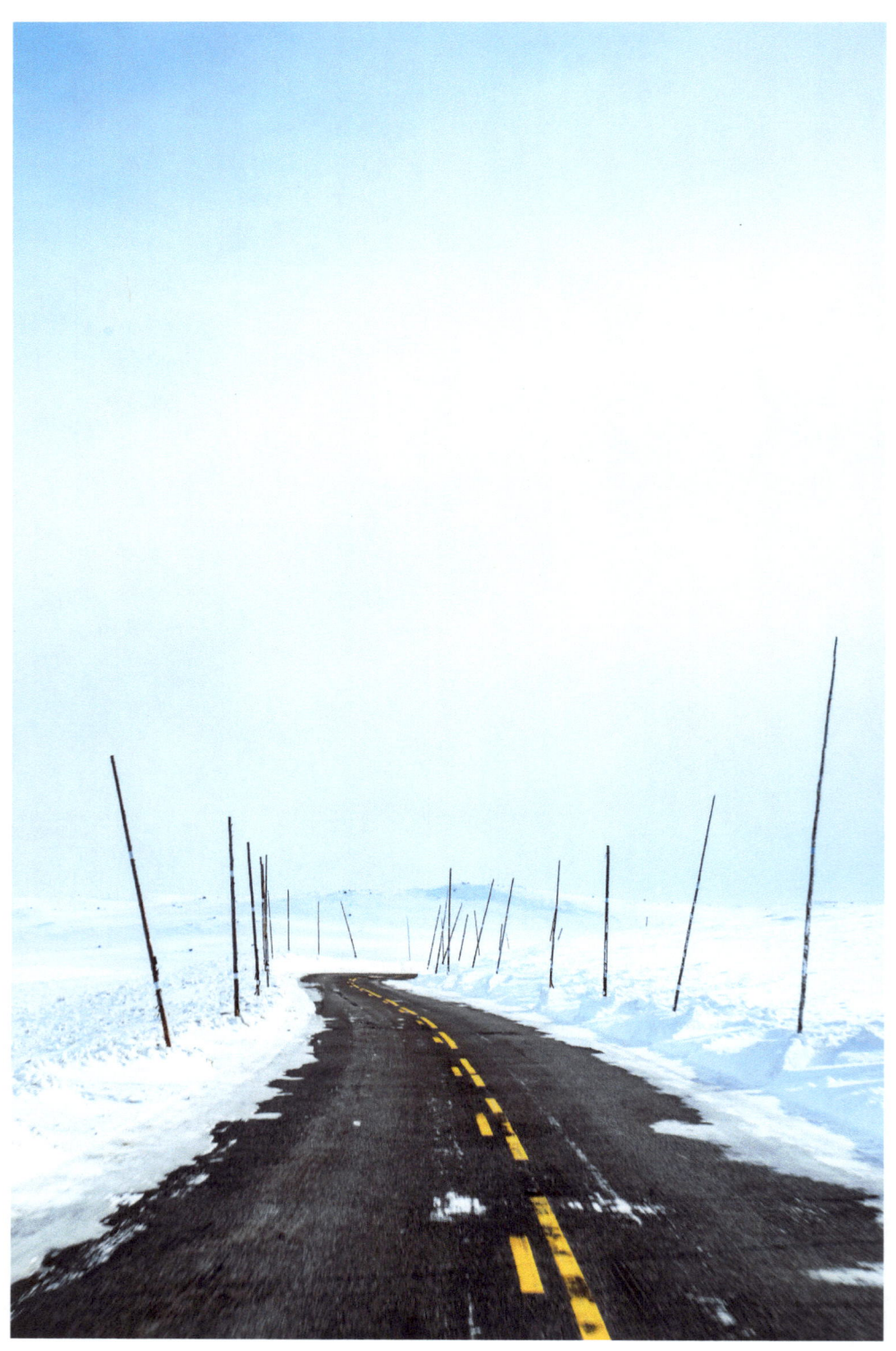

Geilo, Norway

AUTHOR BIO

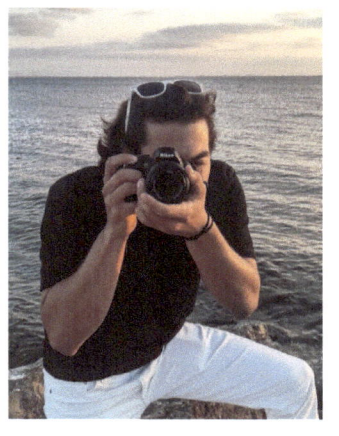

Andy Piñeiro Romero, a multi-dimensional individual with an insatiable curiosity, and a passion for life.

Born in La Habana, Cuba Andy's passion for exploration has taken him on a journey of self-discovery, where he has worn many hats, played many roles, and seen the world through a kaleidoscope of perspectives. He has travelled extensively, immersing himself in the culture and traditions of each place he visits.

Today, Andy is a writer, a photographer, and a true Renaissance man. He has dedicated his life to sharing his experiences, his knowledge, and his insights with the world, and to inspiring others to explore their own potential. To learn more about Andy and his works, visit his website at www.AndyPineiro.org